From Sorrow To Serenity

Meditations For Those Who Have Suffered Pregnancy Or Infant Loss

Susan Fletcher

HUNTER HOUSE PUBLICATIONS
CEDAR RAPIDS · IOWA

From Sorrow To Serenity: Meditations For Those Who Have Suffered Pregnancy Or Infant Loss

Printed in the United States of America

Cover Photo by Chuck Kaloustian
Cover Photo taken at Ushers Ferry Historic Village, Cedar Rapids, Iowa

Library of Congress Number 98-093025
ISBN 0-9662769-1-4

Printed in the United States by:
Morris Publishing 3212 East Highway 30 Kearney, NE 68847

For my little ones
in the arms of Jesus . . .

Sarah Rebecca
James Alan
Susan Elizabeth
James Peter
John Robert
Roberta Ann

Acknowledgments

From Sorrow to Serenity has been, in many ways, a process of planning, preparation, birth and delivery. It would not have been possible without the help of many others in my life. Throughout the past several years, I've been privileged to meet bereaved parents who have shared with me about the loss of their babies. Through their stories, they have reinforced that our God is a caring, loving and healing God. These resilient moms and dads showed much courage, strength and hope in the midst of their grief.

Many thanks go to Helen Hunter for her support and helpful advice, Billie Parr for her care and diligence in editing the final manuscript and Roxanne Rustand, a friend who also walks with me as a bereaved parent, for her encouragement, suggestions and insight.

It is not without sacrifice that this book has come into existence. Not only the sacrifice of my six babies, but also the sacrifice of my family. Thank you to my husband and two living sons for allowing me the time to bring this book to life, especially in the final months. Their support and prayers are appreciated.

Many times as I wrote, I relied on the Holy Spirit to guide me in choosing the right scripture verse and words that would hopefully bring healing to those who read these pages. I am thankful for God's grace and the gift of his son, Jesus the Christ, for blessing this project.

To God be the glory!

Contents

Like many married couples, when my husband and I decided to begin our family, we naturally assumed we would be parents of a beautiful, bouncing baby within a year. And after one year of trying to conceive, we were ecstatic to discover I was pregnant.

But our first pregnancy was not to be. I soon began experiencing severe abdominal and pelvic pain. Doubled over and no longer able to stand by myself, I was rushed into emergency surgery. The doctor's suspicions were confirmed—ectopic pregnancy. Along with a ruptured fallopian tube, came the death of our first baby.

We were thrown into a new world of loss, trying to understand what, in fact, we did lose. Most of our family and friends were more concerned with my physical health. I had undergone major surgery and had encountered severe blood loss from internal bleeding. Few mentioned the fact I had been pregnant and that we were anticipating a new life. Our hopes and dreams for our first child had been shattered.

During the seven years that followed our first loss, my husband and I rode the emotional roller coaster of secondary infertility. We continued to seek treatment to conceive and pursue a successful pregnancy. It was a time of frustration, despair and searching. Yet, we continued to be hopeful.

With each succeeding pregnancy, we tried to remain optimistic. But in the end, my five additional pregnancies never went full term. All lost in the first trimester, our little ones went straight to be with Jesus.

In the midst of those seven years of loss, grief and mourning, came unbelievable blessings. Our two sons by adoption were born and placed in our arms. It was humbling to realize they would not have been a part of our family if the pregnancies had been successful. We give thanks to God and their birthmothers for their loving, unselfish gift to us.

In looking back, I wish there would have been resources available to help us work through our grief. When we lost our first baby, there were few books available about pregnancy or infant loss. And books written from a Christian perspective were even fewer.

Over the past several years, I have been led and encouraged by family and friends to write a book of meditations. Especially for bereaved parents who have suffered a pregnancy or infant loss. Thus, *From Sorrow to Serenity* was born.

You'll notice the book is divided into five sections. *Sorrow* is the beginning point when we are thrown into the unknown, frightening world of grief. *The Journey* takes the reader through the valley of mourning. *Serenity* moves the bereaved from darkness into the light of God's peace. *Special Days* contains meditations for holidays and the anniversary of a loss. The final section, Resource Centers, lists resources available for bereaved parents.

As I write this, the magnolia tree outside my window is laden with beautiful blossoms. I wish that it would remain that way all summer with its pale, pink flowers. Yet I know the blossoms must fall, so the tree will flourish. And so must we, having encountered death and grief, let our "mourning blossoms" give way for new growth to occur in our lives.

For all who have walked the road of unspeakable grief from the death of a baby, may God grant you comfort, healing and hope. In the midst of your sadness, may you find strength, patience and peace as God brings you out of your sorrow and into serenity.

—*Susan Fletcher*

Sorrow

Jesus wept.

John 11:35 NEB

Sorrow

How long must I bear pain in my soul, and have sorrow in my heart all day long? *Psalm 13:2 NRSV*

At the moment our baby is taken from us, a myriad of emotions begin to overshadow our hearts and souls. We are cast into unbelievable shock that can lead to intense denial and anger.

Thus begins the moment of our sorrow. While we cling to the hopes and promises of our faith, we must somehow recognize the reality of our unfair loss. Grieving the loss of a baby is not easy. And anyone who tells you differently has not been there before.

We wish we could neatly check off the emotions and grief stages as we pass them by. But we are not given that luxury, nor the option to choose. We have been unwillingly thrown into the most awful circumstance of our lives.

No matter where you are in the process of grieving the loss of your baby, it is perfectly normal to feel a wide range of emotions. Sorrow, denial, bargaining, anger, even a sprinkling of smiles and laughter from time to time, will invade your soul. And the "what if" questions you may ask are common.

How long must we bear pain in our souls? Like the checklist of grief, we wish we could point our finger on the calendar and declare, "This is the day I will grieve no more." Unfortunately, grief has its own time schedule. Dear sisters and brothers, be gentle with yourselves as you begin to experience grief. Everyone mourns differently, so it is vital you do not compare yourself to another. And please know that your pain and sorrow will not last forever.

Lord, when will my heart and soul be free of sorrow and pain?
I'm afraid I will feel like this forever. Amen.

Sorrow

Bitterly she weeps in the night, tears run down her cheeks; she has no one to bring her comfort among all that love her.

Lamentations 1:2a NEB

How totally isolated I feel in the midst of death. Unending tears flow. So many tears, I don't understand how my body continues to release them. Where are they coming from?

My physical, emotional and spiritual senses are numb. Yet my entire body is enveloped in pain. Nothing is left untouched. I exist each day by going through the motions like a robot.

Silently I scream that no one understands me. Who can bring me comfort? My husband is distant, perhaps dealing with his own pain. My family is concerned only with my physical health, and my friends don't know what to say. They have stopped calling.

And God, where are you? How could a god exist that lets babies die?

All I want is what has so cruelly been taken from me. All I want is my baby, any baby, in my arms.

Are you crying with me God? I'm so alone. Are you out there somewhere? Please let me know you are there. Amen.

Sorrow

I called on your name, O Lord, from the depths of the pit; you heard my plea, "Do not close your ear to my cry for help, but give me relief!" *Lamentations 3:55, 56 NRSV*

It's not fair, God! Why do you create life only to quickly take it away? What is your purpose in all of this?

Don't you know how difficult it is on this pregnancy roller coaster ride? Soaring happy and hopeful one day, only to descend into utter despair when pain and bleeding appear.

I don't know if I want to be this vulnerable again, to be taken for another ride. I don't want to be hurt again, and I don't know if I can trust again.

I do know I have been cheated . . . from another life, another dream.

From the depths of my pain and sorrow I look to you, O Lord. Listen, as I cry out to you in my despair. Amen.

When they call to me, I will answer them; I will be with them in trouble. *Psalm 91:15 NRSV*

"God! Oh, God! It can't be true! There must be a mistake!"

"I'm sorry," says the doctor. "I can't find a heartbeat." The heart that was beating only yesterday is now silent.

My mind and heart race and throb with pain. This can't be happening. This wasn't supposed to happen.

"Would you like to contact your family?" the nurse asks. "Yes. No. I don't know what to do." Sudden shock turns to sobs of anguish.

All I can fathom right at this moment is the pain. Who can help me?

Can you help me, Lord? Your Word says that when I call to you, you will answer. Help me hear your voice. Amen.

For my thoughts are not your thoughts, nor are your ways my ways, says the Lord. . . . so are my ways higher than your ways and my thoughts than your thoughts. *Isaiah 55:8, 9 NRSV*

Okay, Lord. I have many questions. I want answers, and I want them now.

Why did you allow the baby to live within my womb for nine months while everything seemed to be going according to plan? Why was I overdue in delivering the baby? Why didn't my doctor insist on a cesarean section? Why didn't I? If a C section had been performed, maybe my baby would be alive today.

Why was there nothing but silence and stillness at the moment of my baby's birth?

Why, Lord, why?

In searching for answers to my questions, Lord, help me realize that any earthly answer is unacceptable. Help me understand that even if I had all the answers it would not ease my pain. Help me accept this mystery of life and death. Amen.

Sorrow

When we are too weak to have any faith left, he remains faithful to us and will help us. *2 Timothy 2:13a TLB*

I thought my faith was strong, Lord. I innocently believed I could weather any storm that came my way. Now I'm not so sure. Grief has washed over me like nothing I've experienced before in my life. And a shroud of sadness has drained me of strength, feeling and faith.

My days are difficult, Lord. No one seems to notice or care. I am tired when I awake in the morning. And though exhausted at the end of the day, it's hard to sleep. Even my dreams won't let me escape the terrible reality of death.

I think about my baby all the time. Where can I go, Lord? Who can I turn to?

In my desperation I look to you, Lord. Fill me with your strength. Amen.

When my heart was embittered I felt the pangs of envy.
Psalm 73:21 NEB

I am so angry. Today I discovered a friend is expecting her third baby. Wait a minute, God. I am supposed to be pregnant. My baby was to be delivered in two months.

Am I missing a piece of the puzzle, Lord? I am still trying to have one successful pregnancy. When will it be my turn to experience a happy, uneventful pregnancy other women enjoy?

Forgive me, Lord, but secretly I wish all women had to endure what I have endured. I wish every parent understood the frailty of life, what most take for granted. Maybe then they would understand what I am going through.

Lord Jesus, I admit I'm envious, even angry at times. I know you became angry, too. Help me work through my feelings of jealousy, envy and anger and surrender them to you. Amen.

Emptiness, all is empty.

Ecclesiastes 1:2b NEB

All day long I am bombarded with images of babies. There is an endless round of diaper commercials blaring from the television. Happy couples push their little ones in strollers at the mall. Pregnant women and babies are everywhere. Even the special parking space for "pregnant or new moms" is off limits. The nursery, with its rocking chair, crib and neatly arranged changing table, is empty.

The world is full of babies—except my world. I try to scream, but the deep place where my wailing erupts is void. All I feel is emptiness.

My womb is empty. My heart is empty. My arms are empty. Who can restore me again?

I'm so empty, Lord. Will this emptiness ever go away? Please replace my emptiness with your love. Amen.

Sorrow

May those who sow in tears reap with shouts of joy.

Psalm 126:5 NRSV

Could the psalmist's words be true? That those of us who have been thrown into the pit of death and grief will someday shout for joy? How could we ever be joyful again when our babies have died? It is difficult to imagine, isn't it?

Yet one of the most important ways to work toward joy in our lives is to cry. As you continue to grieve over the death of your baby, let your tears flow. Don't hold back. Acknowledge them for the gift they are—God's gift to you.

Your tears can begin to wash away pain, hurt and suffering. Yes, your tears are healing. Let them flow.

Father, thank you for the gift of tears. May the tears I shed over the loss of my baby begin to work a healing in me. Amen.

But now he is dead; . . . Can I bring him back again? I shall go to him, but he will not return to me. *2 Samuel 12:23 NRSV*

The poem began, "I'm just a little feller who didn't quite make it there; I went straight to be with Jesus but I'm waiting for you here . . . ."

I never questioned what happened to my baby's soul after she died. Do miscarried babies go to heaven? Could they? Would they be allowed to enter?

The words of *A Baby's Secret* spoke to me in a new and wonderful way. It was as if God sent angels to guide my hand to this particular book of poems in the church library that day. Powerful words spoke to the very core of my soul, bringing me comfort and peace and tears:

"So sweet Mommy don't you sorrow,
Wipe those tears and chase the gloom,
I went straight to Jesus' bosom
from my lovely mother's womb.

Thank you for the life you gave me,
It was brief, but don't complain,
I have all of heaven's glory
Suffered none of earthlings pain.

Daddy gave me something for you,
It's our secret, Mommy dear,
Pressed it tight against my
forehead
Whispered in my tiny ear,

I'll be waiting for you, Mommy–
You and Daddy, Bud and Sis.
I'll be with you then forever–
Then I'll give you Daddy's kiss.
—J. C. Brumfield

Holy Spirit, how wonderful your timing when you send comforting words to us at a time when we least expect them. Amen.

O Lord, you have examined my heart and know everything about me. *Psalm 139:1 TLB*

When we put on our "I'm fine" mask of outward calmness, we may be able to hide our pain and sadness from others. But this verse from Psalm 139 tells us the Lord knows us in a very intimate way. We can't hide anything from him. In fact, he knew us as we were being formed in our mothers' wombs.

The Lord, in his infinite wisdom and overwhelming love for us, desires a close, personal friendship. Yet, we need to be brutally honest with him. He wants to hear from you. Shout, scream, cry with every fiber of your soul. Confide your anguish of despair, your longing to hold your baby in your arms.

Go ahead. He's listening.

Hear my cries, O Lord. I've stuffed my emotions inside for too long. I want to release them and give them to you. Amen.

Sorrow

The heart of the wise is in the house of mourning;
Ecclesiastes 7:4a NRSV

One of the best descriptions I've ever heard concerning the different stages of grief—shock, denial, anger, acceptance—and how we move about them, is to equate them to the rooms in a house.

Your house or apartment contains different rooms—living room, kitchen, bedroom, etc. And assuming you're not a couch potato, you move from one room to another throughout the day.

Working through the stages of grief is like living in our house. It would be neat and nifty if, when we begin our grief work, we start at the top of the list, travel through each stage, and check them off our list as we struggle on our journey. That's the ideal way to work through grief. It's also the unrealistic way. And unfortunately, that's not how any of us work through our grief. We may find ourselves moving quickly ahead, feeling confident we're making progress, when wham! We're hit by heavy winds, pushing us back into the stage of anger.

Just as we move from room to room in our homes every day, don't be surprised when you move from grief room to grief room. It's natural. It will happen. And when you experience a "setback," don't become discouraged or upset. This is God's way of gently letting you know you may have more issues to face and work through.

What room are you living in today?

Lord, continue to be with me as I move about my many rooms of grief. Thank you for your Word that reminds me it is a wise heart who seeks to mourn. Amen.

Why is my pain unceasing, my wound incurable, refusing to be healed?
Jeremiah 15:18a NRSV

Lord, I thought I would be over this by now. At least that's what my friends and family tell me. But all I can think about is my baby. I still feel the softness of her skin brushed against my cheek. And her sweet smell. Just walking past the nursery kindles my memory of her essence.

I miss my baby so much, Lord. You see, I've never lost anyone before. How am I supposed to react? No one around me knows how to respond either. In their attempt to help, more pain is caused by thoughtless remarks.

Sometimes I find myself rocking in the rocking chair, tightly clutching my baby's blanket. Sometimes I fantasize she's with me. And I'm holding her, rocking her, singing tender lullabies. Only my sobs of pain and aching heart return me to cruel reality—my baby's gone and she's not coming back.

Please tell me, Lord, am I going crazy?

Hear my cries for help, Lord. My arms ache with emptiness and nothing can fill the void I feel at this moment. Amen.

A gentle tongue is a tree of life.

Proverbs 15:4a NRSV

Most couples recite traditional wedding vows when they marry. Perhaps you spoke the following on your wedding day—"in sickness and health . . . for better or worse."

Experiencing the death of your baby—whether by ectopic pregnancy, miscarriage, stillbirth or infant loss—definitely throws you in one of the "worst" stages of your marital relationship.

In the midst of our grief, harsh, misspoken words can erupt from our lips. Sometimes, even as we speak them, we immediately regret what we've said.

As you cope each day, conquering your pain and sorrow, be aware that wisely chosen words bring healing and growth. Don't be afraid to let your spouse know your thoughts, concerns and feelings. Honest, prayerful communication will help strengthen your bonds of love and care.

Father God, thank you for my spouse. May only kind, uplifting words of comfort pour forth from my mouth to bless my marriage. Amen.

In the day of my trouble I call on you, for you will answer me.
Psalm 86:7 NRSV

O Lord, there have been many times in my life when I have been in trouble. Like the time I broke the garage window with the tennis ball. Or skipped class and got in trouble with both the teacher and my parents. Yet, those were childish things.

But today, Lord, my entire being is troubled. I am in distress. For a part of my soul has left, gone from my sight.

My baby has died. Utter darkness and emptiness scream forth from the pit of my soul. Who can I turn to? Who can I call upon for help?

I want to believe your Word, Lord. Tell me, can I truly believe and trust these words of David? You answered your servant David in his time of distress. If I call upon you, Lord, will you answer me?

I hurt, Lord. Help me reach out to you in trust, knowing you will hear and answer.

Dear Lord, it's so hard to trust when an innocent life has been taken away. Fill me with your love and presence so I know you are with me. Amen.

He gives the barren woman a home, making her the joyous mother of children. *Psalm 113:9 NRSV*

After a year of trying to conceive, I was ecstatic to discover I was indeed pregnant. To lose the baby soon after, threw me again into a state of barrenness. Barren. Just the sound of the word rang hollow. My womb was empty. And there was emptiness in my heart and soul as well.

This verse from the Psalms, though, is especially meaningful for me. My sister lovingly quoted this scripture to me after my first loss. This was the first, among many scriptures, that I clung to for hope. Hope that my future would include babies that wouldn't die in my womb. Babies that I would someday rock, cuddle and sing lullabies to.

Is your heart barren? Trust Jesus to fill your emptiness with his comfort and love. Feel his gentle embrace surround you today with healing and hope.

I want to trust in your promises, Jesus. It's difficult when I'm so empty. Please pour out your love to me. Amen.

Where then is my hope? Who will see my hope?

Job 17:15 NRSV

When a friend or family member dies, we have many memories with which to remember them. We gather those memories and place them in our hearts.

But when a baby dies, there are few, if any, tangible memories at all. You may have been able to hold your baby, take pictures or snip a lock of hair. If you experienced an early loss you may have very little or nothing to place in your baby's memory box. Perhaps an ultrasound picture is all that remains of your little one.

We grieve for our dead baby—the loss of hopes and dreams of our gone–but–not–forgotten child. We grieve over the loss of all the "firsts" of childhood—cutting her first tooth, taking his first step, climbing up the steps of the school bus for the first time.

Share with Jesus the hopes and dreams you had for your baby. Let him comfort and soothe your soul as you pour out your heart to him.

Dear Jesus, I feel cheated because I will never experience all the "firsts" with my baby. Please help me as I wrestle with my grief. Amen.

Sorrow

I will speak in the anguish of my spirit; I will complain in the bitterness of my soul. *Job 7:11 NRSV*

There are times when we have the mistaken idea we can't or shouldn't speak our mind—especially as a member of the body of Christ. And no one really wants to hear us complain. But as today's scripture verse tells us, there *will be* times when the agony of our spirit needs to be expressed.

Yet how do we go about speaking the truth of our innermost bitterness and sorrows? Can we "bare all" to anyone who asks how we're doing? It is a wise, discerning friend who allows us to speak honestly about our emotions. Such friendships are blessings from God.

Is there someone in your life right now you can confide in? If not, then who can you turn to? Turn to the same God which Job sought while in his trials of suffering and distress.

Now is not the time to restrain yourself. Our loving, understanding God is listening for your voice.

O God, the pit of my stomach churns with bitterness. Can you hear my cries of anguish? Please comfort me as I cry out to you. Amen.

A sword will pierce your own soul too.

Luke 2:35b NRSV

Simeon's prophecy was amazing and perhaps confusing to Mary. What exactly did God have in store for her firstborn son, Jesus? It would not be until many years later that Simeon's words would be fulfilled. Mary *would* grieve the rejection and death of her son.

When our baby dies, we become part of a distinct group—the bereaved. There is only one price for admission into this group. But what a price to pay. The common bond of death melds us together as one when we mourn. Like Mary, our hearts are pierced with the sword of death.

When you feel sorrowful, alone and helpless, remember Mary. The mother of our Lord also endured heartache over the death of her son, Jesus—just as we now suffer the loss of our babies.

Lord Jesus, I am suffering. Please heal my broken heart. Amen.

They sat with him . . . for they saw that his suffering was very great. *Job 2:13 NRSV*

It was the Jewish custom to remain silent with a friend who was in mourning. Only until after the grieving person spoke, could the other person then speak. Perhaps we could learn something from this tradition today.

How have family and friends responded to you in your grief and mourning? Have they offered quick fix responses by quoting scripture or pat answers such as, "Well, it's for the best." (How could losing my baby be for the "best"?) or "You can always have another." (I wanted this baby, and it's difficult for me to conceive.) or "You weren't that far along—you'll get over it." (I will never forget my baby.)? Yes, insensitive remarks are spoken, because they forget that "it" was your baby.

When others try to comfort us, it seems they feel the need to say *something*. Maybe with their words, our circumstances will change or relief will come. Yes, there is a time to speak words of comfort and truth. But there is also a time when the most important thing we can do for each other is to simply just "be" there for one another.

If you have experienced hurtful, insensitive words, remember Job's friends. They too tried to help. Their hearts were in the right place, even if their words were not.

Father God, surround me with understanding family and friends. Help them walk and wait silently with me. Amen.

Precious in the sight of the Lord is the death of his faithful ones.
Psalm 116:15 NRSV

With her dark curly hair and deep blue eyes, Rachel was a beautiful, happy baby. At her three-month old check-up, the pediatrician announced Rachel was healthy and growing right on schedule. Rachel's parents thought nothing could be better in their lives at that moment.

That was until the afternoon Rachel's mother went to wake Rachel from her nap. In the silence of the nursery, came the awful discovery. Tiny breaths had stopped. Quickly and quietly, sudden infant death syndrome (SIDS) had snatched their daughter. And Rachel's parents were changed forever.

Surrounded by shock and unending questions of "Why?" and "How could this have happened?", Rachel's parents believed they would never recover from their broken hearts. A heaviness of guilt descended upon them. It was difficult to accept comfort from many of their family and friends.

If your baby died from SIDS, be assured there was nothing you did or did not do to cause the death of your baby. Seeking answers to your "What if?" questions will only cause you continued heartache. Nor will they bring any definitive answers.

When babies die and our hearts are broken beyond belief, there are times we can only turn to the One who can and will bring us peace. Take comfort in knowing your faithful little one is precious in the sight of the Lord.

Can you hear my screams of pain and agony, Lord? Can you mend my broken spirit? Amen.

Let the little children come to me, and do not stop them; for it is to such as these that the kingdom of God belongs.

Luke 18:16 NRSV

My husband and I sat quietly in the pathologist's office. Just a few days earlier we had lost our fifth baby to another ectopic pregnancy. Looking through the microscope, we saw what the doctor described to us as degenerative placental tissue mixed among the blood cells—our baby.

And I thought, this is my baby's burial place on two microscopic slides. No formal service, no one singing "Children of the Heavenly Father," no one praying the Lord's Prayer. Yet even if the baby hadn't lived long enough to warrant a funeral, I know where my baby is. He's not filed away indefinitely in some drawer on a slide. He is with you, Father.

In the midst of my confusion, questions, hurt, anger and sadness, I know you are with me; saddened and grieving also. Father, thank you for the life you lent us. Even though that life was out of place within my body, it wasn't out of place in my heart and soul.

As we leave the pathology lab, silently I say good-bye to you, little one, and place you back in Jesus' arms.

Lord God, thank you for the promise of never leaving me, for holding me up when I want to fall so low. Thank you for including my little ones in your kingdom. Amen.

Sorrow

A voice was heard in Rama, wailing and loud laments; it was Rachel weeping for her children, and refusing all consolation, because they were no more. *Matthew 2:18 NEB*

The description of Rachel weeping and wailing brings a vivid picture to mind. Even today, Middle Eastern women still wail loudly and publicly over the death of a loved one, just as Rachel did thousands of years ago.

Unfortunately, in western society, we are encouraged and sometimes told to "hide" our emotions. No one wants to be embarrassed by our visible display of feelings. I've often wondered if Americans took a cue from the Rachels of the world, if we wouldn't be healthier—emotionally, physically and spiritually.

God wants to hear and see our innermost emotions revealed. Have you screamed or wailed to God in mourning the loss of your baby? Do you feel you need to scream? Turn up the radio, take an extra long shower, or take a drive to the country. Let loose! Bring forth your loud, gut-wrenching screams, cries, moans, sobs and laments. Be free to grieve. And then rest in his presence.

Father, I've hidden my emotions for too long. Please take my hurts and replace them with your healing and consolation. Amen.

Sorrow

They shall mourn for him . . . each family by itself;
Zechariah 12:10b-12a NRSV

Aaron and his sister, Bethany, eagerly awaited their new baby brother or sister. While Aaron hoped for a brother, Bethany was happy she wouldn't be the "baby" any longer. Excitement grew as Mom and Dad left hurriedly for the hospital.

But something went terribly wrong. When Mom came home from the hospital, her arms were empty. Jonathan, their baby brother, had lived only a few moments after his birth. Now Aaron and Bethany were sad and confused. Their Mom only cried more when they asked, "Why did God let our baby die?"

Do you have other children at home? If so, it's important to recognize that your children's grief will be different from yours. To you, they may not seem to grieve at all. At least on the outside. Behavioral problems may not surface for several months or years.

What can you do to help? Be open with your children. Let them see your emotions. Answer their questions as honestly as you can, to fit their age and maturity level. And if necessary, seek counseling.

Remember, they are also grieving the loss of their baby. As you mourn, continue to talk, share, play and pray together.

Holy Spirit, comfort my family. Give us hope as we mourn together. Amen.

I will look to the Lord, I will wait for the God of my salvation; my God will hear me. *Micah 7:7 NRSV*

With a spirit of conviction, Micah uses action words. He doesn't write he "might look to the Lord" or he "might wait for God." Micah declares he *will* do these things, confident that his God will hear him.

Amidst the pain of losing a baby, we sometimes unconsciously shut out the people in our lives that want to help us the most. For whatever reason, we may crawl into our shells, not wanting to ever reappear. We block the outside world, feeling safe in our cocoons.

But when we hide, we can't communicate. We remain silent. And disappointment arises when family and friends don't meet our unspoken expectations. We longingly look to them for support, waiting for their help. When it doesn't happen, anger, bitterness and resentment may follow.

It is important you continue to ask the people you love for their help, care and concern. God has placed them in your life as his servants. But also remember the One who never wavers. Take action. Look and wait for the God of your salvation today.

Holy God, help me in my grief. Give me patience as I wait and struggle during my sadness. Amen.

Sing, O barren one who did not bear; burst into song and shout, you who have not been in labor! *Isaiah 54:1 NRSV*

With our sixth and final pregnancy, my husband and I desperately wanted to believe this time would be different. We remained hopeful and optimistic. But as my HCG levels continued to drop, we silently knew the outcome. We prepared for the worst.

It was a difficult time. My body had reached its limit as to what I could physically continue to endure. I had already lost one fallopian tube. My mental health was on the verge of collapse. I couldn't keep putting myself through the unending pain and loss. And my physical health was in danger with each succeeding pregnancy.

And so we made the most painful decision in our marriage. There would be no more pregnancies. The hope of ever having a successful pregnancy and birth was gone forever—cruelly taken away, just like our six babies. Only by the grace of God and pastoral counseling did I survive.

Because of your circumstances, have you, too, come to the place of complete and total loss? Are you faced with the knowledge you will never be able to conceive and bear children again? Please know you have permission to grieve, not only for your baby who has died, but also for the death of your fertility.

Lord, I don't want to bear this pain and heartache. Why have you taken the hope of future children away from me? Please help me understand and accept this suffering. Amen.

Sorrow

I was left all alone—

Isaiah 49:21b NRSV

I met her through a friend. She was young, single and depressed. When Tina first discovered she was pregnant, she panicked. How could she raise a baby by herself? Her boyfriend, whose only solution was abortion, had left. But her family didn't abandon her. With their help and support, Tina began to look forward to her pregnancy and baby.

That was, until her miscarriage. Now confused and sorrowful, Tina had a difficult time coping with her loss. Guilt was written over her heart in bold letters. And although Tina had begun counseling, she couldn't forgive herself. She felt certain God had punished her for having sex before marriage.

If you are single and grieving the loss of your baby, know that there is love and mercy through Jesus. As you weep, he weeps. His forgiveness and grace are yours. Ask him to be with you now.

Lord Jesus, please care for me as you care for my baby. Help me to know you are goodness, light and love. Amen.

Sorrow

Come to me, all you that are weary and are carrying heavy burdens, and I will give you rest. *Matthew 11:28 NRSV*

Before your loss, did you know someone whose baby had died? If so, how did you react? It's difficult to understand the depth of loss and pain until we, too, walk the same path. I remember when a friend suffered a miscarriage and my insensitivity toward her. To shrug off her loss as a non-event, with the typical reply, "You can have another," now makes me ashamed.

The loss of a child is one of the most difficult experiences you will face in life. And it's even harder when the child is a baby or dies in the womb. Why? Because babies simply aren't supposed to die.

The burden of losing a baby is tragic and heavy. We carry many hurts in our baggage of "burdens." Regret, anger, unforgiveness, worry, anxiety, sleeplessness and guilt are just a few.

What burdens are you carrying today? Can you give them to Jesus?

Jesus, your Word says that your yoke is easy and your burden is light. Take my burdens, Jesus. They're too heavy for me. Amen.

A friend is a loving companion at all times.

Proverbs 17:17a NEB

When I think back on the six babies my husband and I lost, and the experience that brought into our lives, I'm reminded of the care and kindness received from friends.

Many friends were sisters in Christ who shared the anguish of infertility, yet reached out of their own pain to lovingly minister to me. Even when the casseroles stopped coming, their help and encouragement continued. It might have been visits to the hospital. Or a cordless phone to use at home after a major surgery. Or being pampered with a manicure. Sometimes it was a hug accompanied by powerful words, "I'm so sorry. I know this must be difficult for you."

And at other times, I had to let my pride slip away and ask for help.

The next time a friend asks, "Is there anything I can do to help?" don't be afraid to respond with suggestions. Because your friends love you, they want to help you on your road to healing.

Lord, thank you for the friends you place in my life. Bless my special friendships with your love. Amen.

Sorrow

Cast your burden on the Lord, and he will sustain you;
Psalm 55:22a NRSV

When we draw near to the place in our grief where there is nowhere else to turn, we find ourselves at a dead end. Life, for us in the outside world, has ceased. Sure, we go through the motions, arising each day, off to a job that may give us a few respite hours. Hours when a career numbs our loss, grief and despair.

It is when we reach this dead end that we discover we are not in control. If we are brutally honest with ourselves, we will realize we never were in control. When we acknowledge the God of the universe, who has, is and will be in control forever, then we will understand the revelation of God. Through his perfect way and timing, the Holy Spirit prompts us to turn control of our lives over to him.

Have you reached the point of no return? Ask God right now to help turn control of your life over to him. When you do, you will embark on a new and different journey.

Loving Father, I can't live like this anymore. I want a new, different direction for my life. Please help me give my life and the life of my baby over to you. Amen.

The Journey

And the day came
When the risk
to remain
Tight in a bud

Was more painful
Than the risk
It took
To blossom.

Author Unknown

Journey

He who journeys in the dark does not know where he is going. Trust to the light, so that you may become men of light.
John 12:35b, 36a NEB

In preparation for the 1996 summer Olympic Games, the Olympic flame made its long journey from Athens, Greece, across the United States, to its final destination in Atlanta, Georgia. Runners from all over the country carried the lit Olympic torch for a short distance, passing the torch on to the next runner.

There was great excitement where I live. The city had been chosen to "host" the flame overnight. On the night of the torch's arrival, my family and I gathered with thousands of others to welcome the runner and the torch.

Through a sea of bodies in the darkness, came a faint flicker of flame. As the runner approached, the flicker turned into a larger flame. The cheers of the people became deafening.

The Olympic torch reminds me of the light of Jesus. When we journey through the darkness of our pain and sadness, it is difficult to see the path ahead. Whether you carry a flashlight, candle or torch, let that light be the light of Jesus. Let him be your guide through the valley of grief. You don't have to walk alone.

Precious Jesus, you are the light of world. Yet, I'm alone and afraid in my darkness. Please come and light my path and take away my fear. Amen.

The Lord is good, a stronghold in a day of trouble; he protects those who take refuge in him, even in a rushing flood.
Nahum 1:7, 8a NRSV

I have never experienced a flood and the devastation and destruction it brings. Yet many people have. Their homes and businesses have been damaged and destroyed by swollen creeks and raging rivers.

Nahum's vision states the Lord will protect those who are "even in a rushing flood." Whether you have thought in these terms before, we who have suffered pregnancy or infant loss are thrown into the rushing waters.

The act of mourning floods us with new and different emotions, many of which we may have never experienced before. Feelings of loss, pain, hopelessness and anger are a few. And you need to be aware that it is normal to experience these rushing flood waters of grief.

Nahum reminds us of three important promises in our day of trouble: 1) The Lord is good to us; 2) He is our stronghold; and 3) The Lord will protect us when we take refuge in him.

As you journey from sorrow to serenity, have you taken refuge in the God of Nahum? Know for certain our God will keep you safe as you pass through the flood waters of your grief.

Almighty God, I thank you that you care just for me. I walk confidently on my journey, knowing you protect me from all harm. Amen.

These trials are only to test your faith, to see whether or not it is strong and pure. *1 Peter 1:7a TLB*

Lord, you know I didn't want to hear this message today during the pastor's sermon. As the lump in my throat and knot in my stomach grew worse, I wanted to cover my ears and shut out the words. Peter's words reinforced what one "good intentioned" member in the congregation reminded me: "my faith was being tested." I needed support and encouragement from my church family. Yet what I felt was condemnation and a lack of faith.

Before my miscarriage, I tried to be Christ-like, living as Jesus would. I thought my belief in God was strong. Now I'm not so sure.

Lord, does this mean because my baby was taken away, my faith wasn't strong enough or good enough? Help me understand, please.

Lord, while your Word says that you will refine your people, comfort me in the fact that you are not the cause of my loss. Amen.

Show me the path where I should go, O Lord; point out the right road for me to walk. *Psalm 25:4 TLB*

What now, Lord? Since my baby's funeral, all I want to do is visit his grave site. The visits to the cemetery seem to bring the only comfort I experience right now. When I'm there, I can almost feel his presence when I talk to him. Is it right, Lord, that I want—*no, I need*—to spend time there?

My entire being is consumed with this thought—if I can't have my little boy, I want to be pregnant again, RIGHT NOW!

Friends tell me, "Wait. It's too soon to try and conceive." With fear and concern in his voice, my husband asks, "What if *it* happens again?"

Lord, all I know is the empty feeling and craving in my womb. Which way, Lord? What should we do?

Lord Jesus, your ways are always perfect. Help me to know what path to take in my life right now. Amen.

And what is faith? Faith gives substance to our hopes, and makes us certain of realities we do not see. *Hebrews 11:1 NEB*

What are your hopes, your dreams? Is your dream of having a baby still alive? Perhaps you've placed that dream aside and dreamed new dreams—maybe a career change or going back to school. Hopes and dreams keep us alive.

What are the stark realities in your life? Is the harshest reality the fact that your pregnancy ended or your baby died? Has your dream of having children died as well?

When Paul talks about faith, we acknowledge the faith of a savior who will never leave us nor forsake us. This faith reality announces that when we come to Jesus, grief baggage and all, he accepts us for who and what we are. When we confess our sins to him, asking him into our lives, faith reality comes alive! And the reality is Jesus! The reality is eternal life. The reality is the hope we will be reunited with our babies again.

Take time right now to ask Jesus to be your personal Lord and Savior. His outstretched arms are waiting for you.

Jesus, thank you for your promise of everlasting life. Forgive me when I doubt. Help my hopes and dreams become realities. Amen.

Trust in him at all times, O people; pour out your heart before him; God is a refuge for us. Psalm 62:8 NRSV

When I think of a refuge, shelter immediately comes to mind. Yet refuge has other meanings, such as protection and sanctuary. "Sanctuary" can evoke images from worship space in a church to a wildlife preserve.

During war time, soldiers can request sanctuary. Within the confines of "holy" space and the blessing of the pastor, priest or rabbi, the soldier is protected and guarded from outside forces.

On this journey we did not choose for ourselves, we may come to the place where we need to stop for a short while. This "holy" rest stop is our refuge. And it is here we can pour out our innermost thoughts to God.

As you enter your sanctuary today, pour forth your heartfelt emotions to the Lord. Feel his peace wash over you as you rest in his care.

Holy God, you are like a mighty fortress for your people. Thank you for keeping me safe in your arms as I walk this path of mourning. Amen.

In the morning, while it was still very dark, he got up and went out to a deserted place, and there he prayed. *Mark 1:35 NRSV*

I am not a "morning person." Just the thought of getting up "when it is still very dark" makes me want to pull the covers over my head!

While Jesus was here on earth, it was important for him to stay connected with his Father. Before the sun arose, he spent time in prayer. As we continue to walk through the valley of grief, it's important for us to remain linked with the One who journeys with us. Continue to share with Jesus your needs, desires, heartaches, even progress you've made since your baby died.

Do you have a regular, daily time you spend with the Lord? If not, determine today what will work best for you. Remember, it's not the time of day you pray, but taking the time to pray that's important. Jesus doesn't care when or where. He's waiting for you, ready to listen.

Jesus, by your example, you taught your disciples the importance of prayer. Help me seek your face every day. Amen.

Each of you should love his wife as himself, and a wife should respect her husband. *Ephesians 5:33 NRSV*

I was shocked and saddened at the news. Two of the couples from the bereaved parent support group had divorced. Their loss had been too great a burden. The death of their baby, along with other marital problems, contributed to the break-up.

It is disheartening that one in two marriages in the United States today ends in divorce. It is even scarier to realize the divorce rate is higher for couples who experience the death of a child. My friends had been affected greatly by their loss. Now they were among the statistics.

How has your marriage fared since your loss? Are the lines of communication open? Are you able to vent your frustrations with your spouse? Is one of you a buoy while the other an anchor? You need each other for continued support.

If you and your spouse find it difficult to cope with your loss or other issues, now is the time to seek help. Don't wait. Look to your pastor or priest for assistance. Perhaps your doctor can refer you to a family counselor. The key is to take action. Please don't become a statistic.

Heavenly Father, my marriage has been strained. Please restore my relationship with my spouse with your healing love. Amen.

The desert shall rejoice and blossom . . . with joy and singing.
Isaiah 35:1, 2 NRSV

You've just won an all expenses paid vacation! Excited? I know I would be . . . until I discover the destination. The desert. Are you still jumping up and down? Me neither.

Most of us would never choose to travel through the desert. Yet the fact is, we are walking through the desert of mourning during this season of grief. And what can we expect to find?

At first glance, we may see only arid, bleak surroundings. We try to protect ourselves from the blistering heat of day to the chill of night. As we trek on, we thirst for refreshment from an oasis wellspring. Our valley of death is aptly named.

Yet in our tunnel vision, we may overlook the beauty and vitality the desert offers. From the cactus flower in bloom to the jack rabbits running about, the desert teems with life.

What have you overlooked as you travel through the desert? Can you hear the music?

Father, help me see your creation and its beauty even in the midst of my desert heart. Amen.

Journey

Those who walk in wisdom come through safely.
Proverbs 28:26b NRSV

How are you progressing on your journey? Perhaps it's time to take a few moments to stop, rest and reflect.

Are you satisfied where you are today? Maybe you are further along your grief journey than you thought possible. Is your life returning to some "normalcy?" Or have you become stuck in the muck and mire, where every step is difficult and grief continues to pull you down?

You may continue to wrestle with the thought of a future pregnancy. Are you asking yourself some of the following questions? When should we begin again to try and conceive? What will I do if I become pregnant and lose the next baby? Oh God, I can't go through this again. Should we consider adoption?

Searching for answers to our life-changing questions may come from many different sources. It's wise to seek answers to some of your future pregnancy concerns from your doctor. You may find guidance and comfort from your pastor or counselor. Family and friends may also be a source to confirm any future decisions you need to make.

How can we walk in wisdom? By continuing to seek God's face, talking with him and more importantly, listening for his voice. Don't forget to seek wisdom through God's Word. It will continue to be the nourishment you need for your journey.

There have been times I've stumbled on my journey, Lord. Protect me and see me safely through. Amen.

The Lord tests the righteous and the wicked.

Psalm 11:5a NRSV

Like many other happily married couples, life was good for Nancy and her husband. That is, until they lost their twin sons at 20 weeks gestation. Shock and despair rolled in like waves around them. Anger reared its ugly head. Nancy couldn't believe that God would allow this to happen.

Hadn't she been a "good enough" Christian? She wondered if she was being punished and asked the universal question, "Why me, Lord?"

One of the hardest things for Christians to understand is why terrible events happen in our lives. Is God "out to get you" or punish you for something you may have done?

With the truth of David's words, we realize that all are tested; both the righteous and the wicked. Not one of us is exempt. Yet, how we respond to the trials that are thrown upon us, determines where we may be in our spiritual journey.

No one likes to be tested. Especially when the test is coping with the loss of a baby. So be honest with God today. If you haven't shared your anger with him lately, let him know how you feel. Cry, shout, scream. Release those emotions that have been sealed tightly. Don't be afraid. He's listening and waiting with open, loving arms.

Oh God, I don't understand why you've put me through this test. Please help me accept this part of my life's journey so I can continue to walk and grow with you. Amen.

Wait for the Lord; be strong, and let your heart take courage.
Psalm 27:14 NRSV

Waiting. I am tired of waiting. I am tired of waiting for it to be my turn at what everyone seems to take for granted. I continue to wait to become a member of that forbidden, elite group: the sisters of mommyhood. As soon as I am about to be initiated into their sorority—with full rights of membership including the secret handshake—I am given the following instructions: "Please wait."

Yet, have I been waiting for the Lord to answer my prayer in only my way and time? Have I abandoned his perfect timing and plan for my life?

Am I waiting for the perfect time to accept my loss and move on to another stage of my life? Or can I come to the place of waiting on the Lord to become his servant?

Lord, fill me with your strength and courage. Help me understand that when I wait upon you, my soul is renewed by your love and presence. Amen.

For surely I know the plans I have for you, says the Lord, plans for your welfare and not for harm, to give you a future with hope. *Jeremiah 29:11 NRSV*

As I cried, the other women in the Bible study wondered how to respond. I had announced yet another pregnancy, only to realize this little soul would soon be with Jesus and not in my womb. Perhaps they wanted to slip quietly out of the room and not deal with their distraught sister in Christ.

A fellow sister who shared the pain of her loss—infertility—spoke hope-filled Jeremiah words. Another comforted me with hugs and began praying for me. Sobs and oceans of tears gushed from the pit of my soul.

Later that night, I again realized that God himself, the mighty Yahweh, had plans for me. And these plans written by his holy hand were for my well-being, to build me up, not to tear down. He was building a future for me.

At that moment, I stood on the promise of a future that included a living child in my life.

Holy Father, when failure comes into our lives, it is good to be reminded that you promise us good not evil. Today, help me to stand on your promise, no matter what happens in my life. Amen.

I waited patiently for the Lord; he inclined to me and heard my cry. *Psalm 40:1 NRSV*

I can hear the voice of my mother to remain patient and stand still as I waited for her to comb the snarls from my hair. Trying to learn the virtue of patience as a child, or as an adult, is not easy.

In our fast food, fast paced society, patience appears to be in short supply. I patiently waited to conceive and deliver a healthy baby. But in the end, my patience was not rewarded. It seemed my only reward was a slap in the face.

What I lost along the way was God's timing. I had to relearn patience. When I realized I needed to wait upon the Lord, instead of the other way around, I rediscovered that he was still there, heeding my cries and pleas of agony and despair and grief.

Let me not forget, Lord, that you are always present waiting to hear my cry. Amen.

Journey

I am the way, and the truth, and the life.

John 14:6a NRSV

As a child, did you play with building blocks? Those different shapes, sizes and colors of blocks have sparked imaginations, allowing kids to become instant architects and builders. One of my favorite designs to build was a village with a surrounding wall for protection. But with a quick wave of the hand or swift kick of the foot, my village was destroyed, along with its protective wall.

When we mourn, we sometimes build walls around ourselves. Our walls insulate us from insensitive remarks. They protect us from being hurt again. What kind of walls do we place around ourselves? Walls of pain, anger, distrust or fear? Perhaps you have other walls you have built.

As we journey on our way, we are reminded of Jesus' words: *"I am the way, the truth, and the life."* We acknowledge the truth of his existence and resurrection. Because of Jesus, we *can* journey to the cross. And when we arrive, we discover an empty cross. But alleluia! His resurrection is real.

Because of Jesus, we are free and forgiven people. Because Jesus made *the way* for us, we can make our mourning journey. Because Jesus gave us *the truth and the life*, we can travel in confidence, knowing we are not alone.

Then we are free to wave our hand, tear down our self-made walls and allow Jesus to enter in.

Dear Jesus, help me break down these walls I have built. Please replace them with your loving presence. Amen.

So do not worry about tomorrow, for tomorrow will bring worries of its own. *Matthew 6:34a NRSV*

I used to be a "born worrier." I worried about anything and everything in my life. From work to finances to another pregnancy loss. So what changed my attitude?

I learned to put my trust in Jesus instead of the god of worry. Now, this is not to say I still don't become troubled. Of course, I do. Anxiety and worry are a part of human nature. And Jesus' words reflect that we will continue to have trouble.

Yet, when our thoughts are focused on past or future events, we miss out on the present. We know the reality of God's presence, both past and future. But if we never live in the present, we may miss the blessings and mercy God has for us at that *precise moment*.

Have you been worrying about another loss? Give your concerns to Jesus. Don't miss an opportunity to receive God's grace. It's yours. Right here. Right now.

When I am anxious, Jesus, help me remember to trade my worry for your peace. Amen.

Journey

Whoever drinks the water that I shall give him will never suffer thirst any more. *John 4:14a NEB*

If you've ever taken a long driving vacation, you know it's important to pull over, stop and take a break every few hours. Maybe you gas up the car and grab a bite to eat as well.

How about your travels on your grief journey? Have you become tired? Do you need to pull over at the rest stop? Every so often, we do need to stop, rest and refuel. Our minds and bodies need nourishment to help us continue on our trek.

Food and drink will satisfy our physical needs. But more important, we need to refuel our spiritual lives. Taste God's living Word and Water. Jesus is waiting at the rest stop to refresh you. Stop today and be refilled. Let his springs of living water pour over you today.

Thank you, Jesus, for your living water that soothes and restores my soul. Amen.

And he fixed his attention on them, expecting to receive something from them. *Acts 3:5 NRSV*

A week after their son's stillbirth, Sharon and Michael were still outraged at their doctor's lack of response in the delivery room. Without acknowledging their son's death, the doctor simply turned around and walked out. How could their doctor be so cold and callous? Especially when he had greeted them so warmly during their office visits.

When you experienced your loss, how did your doctor respond to your needs? Perhaps your doctor understood your emotional pain and expressed his or her sympathy. We know, however, that not everyone expresses himself the way we would like—particularly during stressful, difficult times. And when we expect a certain response, we set ourselves up for disappointment.

If you felt your doctor wasn't sensitive about your loss, please remember he or she is just like you—"only human." Know that your doctor may be hurting as well, but is unable to show his or her emotions.

If this is an issue that has troubled you, it would be wise to discuss your concerns with your doctor. This is especially true if you continue to have a patient-doctor relationship. In a loving, non-threatening way, let your doctor know how you were hurt. With God's help, then also forgive.

I praise and thank you, Lord Jesus, for those in the medical profession. Help me see my doctor through your eyes. Amen.

Journey

Those who wait for the Lord shall renew their strength . . . they shall walk and not faint. *Isaiah 40:31 NRSV*

Have you ever walked with someone who was always one or two paces ahead of you? I have, and it's frustrating. I would try and take longer strides, which only resulted in strained, sore muscles. Or I'd ask the person to slow down a little. And he would. But gradually, the pace would accelerate again.

As you journey on the path of grief, are you ahead or behind of where you need to be? Please remember, there's no right or wrong answer. It's natural for us to be at different places as we mourn.

This is especially true for couples. Although it is normal for couples to mourn at different rates, relationships may become stressed. Riding the proverbial seesaw, you may be "up" one day, while your spouse is "down." It is important to recognize and understand this aspect of mourning.

But perhaps the better question to ask is this: Are you *waiting* on the Lord? Or have you passed him by? Are you quickly trying to resolve your grief by pushing it aside, not wanting to deal with *it* at all? Are you alone and exhausted?

Our God gives us wonderful directions for our journey. If you find yourself getting ahead of the Lord, slow down and idle in neutral for awhile. Then wait for him to catch up.

Your promises, O Lord, comfort my weary soul. Give me gentle reminders when I'm walking too fast. Amen.

It is the Lord who goes before you. He will be with you; he will not fail you or forsake you. Do not fear or be dismayed.
Deuteronomy 31:8 NRSV

When we become Christians, we sometimes believe our lives will be spared from any and all difficulties. But the simple truth is that no one—believers and non believers alike—is exempt from pain and suffering. All of us experience loss sometime in our lives. It's the fallout of living in a broken, sinful world.

There is another hard reality we must face as well. And that is we may experience other losses in our lives. Future losses may be very trivial. The loss of personal items, such as keys or credit cards, can be replaced. But our precious and special babies cannot.

Our innocence of life died along with our babies. And in its place came the discovery there are no guarantees while on earth.

Centuries ago Moses spoke comforting words to Joshua. Today we also know that whatever the future brings, our Lord will continue to go before us. He will pave the way, no matter where our path leads.

Heavenly Father, as I journey through life, give me reminders of your constant care and concern for me. Amen.

The way of human beings is not in their control, they cannot direct their steps. *Jeremiah 10:23 NRSV*

I like to be in control. Like the captain on a well-run ship, I try to be aware of every detail in my family's life. Church, school, sports, work and volunteer schedules are plotted from the bridge. And this works great until the unexpected happens. The family ship runs smoothly until circumstances beyond our control roll in like a tidal wave.

And again I realize, *I am not in control.* As hard as I try to steer the ship's wheel in the direction I want to travel, I can't. Why is that always so hard for me to remember? When will I ever learn?

The plain truth is that there are some things we just cannot control in life. And one of them is the stark reality that babies die. As fervent as our prayers may have been to save our babies' lives, they ultimately died. And we quickly discovered we could not control their lives in this world.

As you walk this journey, keep asking questions. The Lord will bring peace to your heart as you seek answers to the mysteries of life and death.

Lord, I surrender. Take control of my life and direct my steps to follow you. Amen.

Be filled with his mighty, glorious strength so that you can keep going no matter what happens. *Colossians 1:11 TLB*

Fasting has never been easy for me. A few sips of water help curb the first pangs of hunger. As the day goes by, though, the sounds emanating from my stomach make me realize how hungry I've become.

Without food, our bodies and minds have a difficult time functioning. The same is true if we deprive ourselves spiritually. Feasting on God's Word is one way to keep our spiritual bodies and minds fit. Reading scripture fills our soul with life, strength and purpose.

As you continue your walk through the valley, make a commitment to read your Bible every day. Use a daily devotional book. Or ask the Lord to reveal a special verse for you today. God's Word will fill you with his power to persevere.

Father God, enlighten me with your holy scripture. Breathe new life in me as I read your holy words. Amen.

A time to weep and a time to laugh, a time to mourn.
Ecclesiastes 3:4 NRSV

The first time I met the grieving couple was at their infant son's funeral. Born with multiple birth defects, their first-born had lived only a short while.

My pastor suggested I attend the funeral, to be of some support. After all, I was an experienced "veteran" at this loss business. Perhaps I would know the right words to say at the right time to the young, grieving couple.

Over the next several months, friendship grew between us. We attended a monthly support group for bereaved parents. We shared our stories of pain and agony. Together we shed tears of sorrow and tears of joy when new life arrived.

We became soul sisters and brothers in Christ.

Is there a support group available to you? If so, consider being a part of a group with others who walk the same journey as you. If not, consider organizing a local group at your church or hospital. It is helpful and healing to cry and laugh with others who share your sorrow and pain.

Father, it is good to share our lives with others you have placed in our path. Thank you for your perfect timing and your help. Amen.

Come away to a deserted place all by yourselves and rest a while.
Mark 6:31a NRSV

Has there ever been a time in your life when you wanted to "throw it all away" and move to a deserted island? I know I have. And I suspect most of us have at one time or another.

When our lives become hectic and frazzled, it's natural for us to want to escape. Our day-to-day responsibilities, however, remind us it would be difficult to leave everyone and everything behind forever.

But let's take our cue from Jesus. When his disciples became overwhelmed by their comings and goings, Jesus knew what they needed most. R & R!

Have you been taking time to rest and relax on your journey? It's important to remember that when you begin to feel stress in your life, listen to the words of Jesus. Come away with your Lord to a deserted place all by yourself and rest a while.

Jesus, thank you for the refreshment you give to my weary and tired soul. After I rest with you, I know my journey can continue. Amen.

And after you have suffered for a little while, God . . . will restore, support, strengthen and establish you.

1 Peter 5:10 NRSV

We like to believe our journeys have a beginning, middle and end. But as we journey through the land of suffering, is the end ever in sight? Have you asked yourself that question since your baby died? Do you feel you are on a mourning treadmill that never stops?

When every fiber of our being aches with loss and pain, it is hard to imagine a life without suffering. One day, however, you will realize you have jumped off the treadmill of grief. Your suffering has subsided, and you begin to feel renewed in God's love.

When we're exhausted from the work of our grieving, it's good to remember the words of Peter. Our journey of loss is but a momentary part of our earthly life. God has promised our suffering will not last forever.

Father God, help me remember that my life on earth is short compared to the time I will spend with you in eternity. Amen.

A good name is to be chosen rather than great riches.
Proverbs 22:1a NRSV

Names are important to us. Our names identify us, tell others who we are, and reflect our personalities and the characteristics of God.

While you were expecting your baby, did you look through "baby name" books, searching for just the right name? Choosing a name is significant. Our names distinguish us throughout our entire lives.

If you knew the gender of your baby, you may have named him or her. If you experienced an ectopic pregnancy or early miscarriage, you may not have known whether your baby was a boy or girl. Some couples choose a name that is appropriate for either sex. Some moms "sense" they were carrying a girl or boy. You can also pray and ask the Holy Spirit to reveal to you the sex of your baby.

Naming your baby helps give identity and meaning to his or her short life. As you name and place your baby back in the arms of Jesus, healing begins.

Jesus, into your arms, I give you (speak your baby's name). Amen.

This is the sign of the covenant that I have established between me and all flesh that is on the earth. *Genesis 9:17 NRSV*

My day had been stressful. Nothing had gone right. Think "Murphy's Law" multiplied a gazillion times and you'll get the picture. By the time I drove home at the end of the day, I was a "basket case." My nerves were shot, I was grouchy and tired and boy, was I angry.

Tears began to well up in my eyes. I tried to keep my eyelids open as high as I could so the tears wouldn't begin to drop. As I tried to see through blurry eyes, I wondered, "How could I still be angry?" Besides, petty things had set my anger button off. Or had they? Was I still harboring unresolved anger in my heart? Did I need to have another heart to heart talk with God about my baby's death?

At that moment, a vibrant rainbow appeared. Tears began to gush like waterfalls from my eyes. And God's promise to Noah flashed across my mind. God had protected Noah and his family from destruction. They had survived. In the beauty and untimely appearance of the rainbow, I felt God's protection.

With his help, I would survive.

Thank you, Father, for placing rainbows in my life when I need them the most. Amen.

You must forgive as the Lord forgave you.

Colossians 3:14 NEB

Along the journey, I've discovered the key to healing. This special key unlocks the door leading to the serenity we're searching for. Your key might be very small and light. Or it may be so heavy and large you have a difficult time holding it in your hand.

A word is engraved on the key. *FORGIVENESS.*

Before we can enter through the door of healing, forgiveness needs to come. Ask Jesus to help you search your heart. Are there family or friends you need to forgive? Is there someone you need to forgive because of their insensitivity about your loss? Perhaps your doctor, pastor, relative or friend? More importantly, do you need to forgive yourself? Or God?

When you come to the locked door, insert your key of forgiveness. The one true healer—Jesus—is waiting on the other side for you.

Jesus, by the power of your Holy Spirit, help me forgive those who have hurt me in the past. Help me forgive myself. Help me forgive you. Amen.

For wisdom is better than jewels, and all that you may desire cannot compare with her. *Proverbs 8:11 NRSV*

In the past, I focused on everything that was missing in my life. I constantly compared myself with family and friends. Not because I lacked a comfortable lifestyle. But because I lacked the one thing I so desperately wanted—a baby.

Looking back now with perfect hindsight, it's much easier to understand the meaning of this verse from Proverbs. When we arrive at the place where the only desire of our heart is the wisdom of God, we realize that all the riches in the world or even relationships, cannot fill our hearts the way God does.

Do you still desire the things of this world? Even that of a child to hold in your arms? When we surrender to Jesus, he brings us to the crossroads of a peaceful heart. It is there and then we desire nothing more than him.

Bring me to your crossroads of peace, Lord Jesus. Fill me with your desire for wisdom. Amen.

By the tender mercy of our God, the dawn from on high will break upon us . . . to guide our feet into the way of peace.
Luke 1:78, 79 NRSV

What a wonderful prophecy! From his once silent lips, Zechariah spoke words of hope. Especially for those of us who "sit in darkness and the shadow of death."

But as we journey, are we still sitting? If so, it's time to stand up and move forward. I know, I can hear you say, "I'm not ready to move. I like it where I am. I'm comfortable." Being comfortable or complacent in our grief, however, will never allow us to grow toward the healing we so desperately need in our lives.

If you are feeling this way, are there unresolved loss issues you need to face? Are you angry at everyone and everything around you? Are you denying your grief, hoping your sorrow will somehow fade away as you ride off into the sunset? Or do you feel guilty, because to move ahead in your healing would somehow deny the existence of your baby? Be honest with yourself as you answer these questions.

As you approach the end of your journey, do you see the light of dawn? The light of Jesus? Take a risk. Stand up and walk forward. Trust the light to guide you in a new direction.

Holy Jesus, give me courage to arise from the darkness. Please guide me with your light. Amen.

Serenity

By the tender mercy of our God,
The dawn from on high will
break upon us,
to give light to those who sit in
darkness and in the
shadow of death,
to guide our feet into the way
of peace.

Luke 1:79 NRSV

Serenity

Neither the pillar of cloud by day nor the pillar of fire by night left its place in front of the people. *Exodus 13:22 NRSV*

God gave the Hebrews a pillar of fire and a pillar of cloud as a compass and for protection in their search of the Promised Land.

As we travel to our "Promised Land" of peace and serenity, God could place clouds and fire before us. Or maybe we would use sophisticated navigational satellites. But there's something better to direct our journey. It's the Bible.

God's presence comes alive in us when we continue to seek him. By reading his Word daily, we fill ourselves with wisdom and contentment.

Your new journey of serenity is just beginning. Don't forget to take along God's road map!

Father God, I praise and thank you for your Word. May it guide me throughout my life. Amen.

The Lord is my strength and my might, . . . and I will praise him.
Exodus 15:2 NRSV

Having passed through our journey of grief, we are physically, emotionally and spiritually drained. We are in need of rest. Yet, the first thing Moses and his people did after escaping from Pharaoh's army was to sing praises to God.

How has your "singing praises to God" been? Perhaps in the past several months you could only cry out to God. In your pain and anguish, God understands. But could your pain now turn into praise to the Holy One of Israel?

Where and how can you begin to praise God? Continue to read Chapter 15 of Exodus. Read David's words in the Psalms. Or listen to praise and worship music. Surround yourself with melodies of heavenly music to soothe your heart.

A worshipful, thankful heart will bring honor and glory to God.

Lord God, you are the strength of my heart. I want to praise you all the days of my life. Amen.

Since he himself has passed through the test of suffering, he is able to help those who are meeting their test now.

Hebrews 2:18 NEB

If you were granted one wish to remove any obstacle, thorn or suffering in your life, what would be your wish? Would it be that your baby had not died or your pregnancy had not ended in miscarriage?

At first thought, we might all say, "Yes, that's exactly what I wish for. Erase the horrible grief I have endured. Take it away and place my baby back in my arms!"

When you reach the path of peace and serenity in your life, acceptance enters into your heart and soul. Acknowledgment of past hurts and grief gives way to acceptance of what has been and will be.

It is at this place where our pain is transfixed into comforting others. It is a mystery of how, in the experience of our pain, we can reach out and help others. As followers of Jesus, we know this is possible only by the power of the Holy Spirit.

Jesus, you are waiting for me to give out of my pain to help others. Thank you for this gift. Amen.

One thing I do know, that though I was blind, now I see.
John 9:25b NRSV

While purchasing a new pair of eyeglasses, I decided to take advantage of the new Transitions® lenses. Perhaps you've heard of them. Like the original photo-gray lens, the Transitions® lens, darkens when exposed to sunlight. It's like having two glasses in one.

When we have walked through sorrow, we sometimes lose sight of everything else going on around us. Our day to day activities become so routine, we don't realize we are functioning at all. And because we are so blinded by our loss, it is hard to see the positives in our lives. We're wearing sunglasses.

Just as Jesus restored the blind man's eyesight, we, too, regain our sight when we are healed of our grief. Our restored vision gives us new understanding of our past. Putting on our transition glasses helps us look back to see the blessings that have come from our loss experience.

Which glasses are you wearing today?

Lord, thank you for restoring my vision. Help me continue to see the light and not the darkness. Amen.

I have learned to be content with whatever I have.
Phillipians 4:11b NRSV

Growing up as a "baby boomer," I was surrounded by all the necessities of life. Of course, there were always the latest Barbie® accessories and doll clothes I thought I couldn't live without. Yet I was content.

Today, however, I struggle for contentment in my life by searching for happiness in the physical and material world. Yet I know in my heart that accumulating "the things of this world" will not bring me lasting joy.

Is your contentment spiritually based or performance based? If we continue to think, "My life will be complete when I have a baby," we're headed for trouble. The contentment we so desperately seek in future children will dissipate when the excitement of having a new baby fades.

So how can we be more like Paul in our search for contentment? Let's continue to focus on what is good in our lives rather than what is painful and missing. Today let's seek contentment from the right hand of God—his son, Jesus.

There are many things I would like in my life, Jesus. Please fill my heart with your contentment. Amen.

For this slight momentary affliction is preparing us for an eternal weight of glory beyond all measure, because we look not at what can be seen . . . *2 Corinthians 4:17, 18 NRSV*

When our baby dies, it's difficult to believe we will ever be able to ascend from the bottomless pit of despair and grief. Darkness surrounds us. And all we "see" is the loss of our baby.

Yet, as we traveled through our grief journey and into a changed life, we realize we have indeed gone from the blackness of the pit into the brightness of day. This is when we begin to see more clearly.

God's Holy Spirit transforms our hearts and minds to "see" our suffering and loss in different ways. His Spirit helps our focus go beyond our earthly afflictions to eternal glories.

How is your vision today? When you begin to look backward, remember Paul's words. Look to the "unseen."

Father, there are times when I still miss my baby. Help me see your unseen promise of hope, healing and eternal life. Amen.

I will rejoice in the Lord; I will be happy in the God of my salvation.
Habakkuk 3:18 TLB

Today a sudden wave of emotion came over me. I laughed. I actually laughed. From a hidden place deep inside came the beginnings of laughter that I thought had died along with my baby.

God has created all of our emotions—joy and sadness, laughter and tears. He has given us the gift of laughter to bring smiles to our faces and warm our souls.

Have you been able to laugh lately? Replace the seriousness in your life with silliness. Listen to a tape of Christian comedians. And get ready to laugh heartily.

Loving Father, thank you for your gift of laughter. Fill me with healing laughs every day. Amen.

The Lord will fulfill his purpose for me; your steadfast love, O Lord, endures forever. *Psalm 138:8a NRSV*

Mary, the mother of Jesus, fulfilled one of God's greatest plans of all time. Though not realizing the full purpose God had for her life, Mary immediately accepted his plan by faith.

What is your purpose in life? Is it to be a good husband or wife? An honest, hard-working employee? A caring friend who shares the love of Christ?

Or is your life's purpose lacking because your arms are empty, wanting and waiting to hold your little babe?

Yes, our hopes and dreams do need to be kept alive. Are you still wishing and planning for a successful pregnancy and healthy baby?

God wants you to share your hopes and dreams with him. Go ahead. Talk to him right now by pouring out your fears and frustrations. Share your hopes and dreams with God. He's listening, waiting to fulfill his purpose in you.

Do you really care for me, Lord? Hear my doubts, my hopes and my dreams. Let your purpose be fulfilled in me. Amen.

Those of steadfast mind you keep in peace—in peace because they trust in you. *Isaiah 26:3 NRSV*

There is a poignant story of how the hymn, *It Is Well With My Soul*, came to be written. On an ocean voyage, Horatio Stafford's daughters were lost at sea. Hoping to find comfort and resolve in his life, Stafford journeyed to the location where his daughters' ship went down. He penned the words to this now familiar hymn while visiting their watery graves.

Trusting God, Stafford allowed his tragedy and grief-stricken heart to be replaced with Holy Spirit healing. Through God, Horatio Stafford's words have brought comfort, healing and peace to countless others since then.

As we continue our voyage in the aftermath of grief and mourning, it is comforting to feel God's presence. Let him surround you with love, hope and peace. Then you will be able to say to yourself and others—

"It is well. It is well with my soul."

Heavenly Father, thank you for the healing gifts of creation and expression you give your people. Amen.

The sufferings we now endure bear no comparison with the splendour, as yet unrevealed, which is in store for us.

Romans 8:18 NEB

It wasn't until after several losses and considerable grief work that I began to appreciate Romans 8:18. As my eyes always searched for Romans 8:28, I overlooked this earlier verse.

Yet, when I discovered this scripture, hope and confidence restored my thirsty soul.

These powerful words were a gentle reminder to me that no matter what circumstances I had experienced or what future losses I might endure, nothing could take away the promise and splendour of eternal life.

And being reunited with my babies once again.

Lord God, I thank and praise you, for your words are a soothing, healing balm to comfort my soul. Amen.

He will wipe every tear from their eyes; there shall be an end to death, and to mourning and crying and pain; for the old order has passed away! *Revelation 21:4 NEB*

This is one of my favorite faith-promise scriptures. When I read these words, a soothing peace washes over me. I often share this verse with friends and acquaintances who have also experienced a loss.

Today's words from John are healing. Perhaps they will have the same effect on you as well.

The book of Revelation gives us hope. Why? Because the pain we've experienced is now overshadowed by the complete and utter joy all Christians will share when Christ returns.

Alleluia! There is reason to be joyful. We know the future. God wins!

Father God, I stand on the promise of your Word. When Jesus returns again, death will no longer rule. Amen.

I will hope continually, and will praise you yet more and more.
Psalm 71:14 NRSV

When my father-in-law died unexpectedly of an aneurysm, the family was thrown into a world of shock. No one had anticipated his early death. We grieved over his death and our loss. As Christians, we rejoiced knowing he was with Jesus.

When our babies die their unexpected deaths, we too, are tossed into turmoil. Denial, anger, even bitterness make their appearance. You know all the emotions.

Yet, at some point there comes a glorious day when darkness gives way to light. The shadow of what has been is put to rest. In its place comes hope. Hope that you can and will make it through another day. Hope that God is walking with you on your new faith-filled journey.

The hope you will see your baby again.

Lord, I want to be like the psalmist. No matter where my journey takes me, I praise you for being a God of hope. Amen.

He reached down from heaven and took me and drew me out of my great trials. He rescued me from deep waters.

Psalm 18:16a TLB

Looking back over the past several months of my life, this verse has taken on new meaning. Only when we experience one of life's greatest trials, do we begin to understand rescue operations.

Once, when my husband and I were on a Windjammer cruise, the weather took a turn for the worse. Hurricane season was almost upon us, and the approaching storm was a warm-up for things to come. As the wind and waves became stronger, the ship tossed and pitched. I became sick, not wanting to leave my bunk in the cabin. When a shipmate came to see if any water was leaking in, I declared I would "go down with the ship" because I was too sick to move. Fortunately, the storm subsided. The ship, crew and green-looking passengers survived.

At that moment of churning seas and stomachs, I would have welcomed anyone plucking me out of the ship and gently landing me on shore.

And that's what it's been like since my losses. I know that at just the right time, my Father in heaven will reach down, pull me to safety and help me face any turbulent storms.

Abba Father, thank you for caring for me as your child. Thank you for your protection in the storms of life. Amen.

There was a calm.

Luke 8:24b NRSV

When you look at a full moon on a clear evening what do you see? Can you find any green cheese or the man in the moon? Among the many craters on the moon, scientists have named one of the largest the "Sea of Tranquillity."

This moon "sea" has no water and waves to be tossed about like the seas on Earth. It is truly peaceful all the time.

Is your heart like the sea of tranquillity? Or is it being tossed about by fierce waves?

Jesus, you calmed the water for your disciples. Calm my fears and heart with your peace when I am tossed about by returning, raging waves. Amen.

It is good to give thanks to the Lord, to sing praises to your name, O Most High; *Psalm 92:1 NRSV*

Traveling on a long journey can tire us, make us cranky and yearn for solitude and nourishment. It is good then, to come to the place in the innermost chamber of our soul where we are at peace with those around us, ourselves and especially God.

And so when we arrive at the place of peace, it seems only fitting to give thanks and praise to the One who has shared the journey with us.

Have you reached the point along your trek where contentment has returned to your life, replacing the hurt, anger and despair?

Praise God for how he has helped you and will continue to sustain you in this place of serenity.

I join the psalmist in praising and giving thanks to you, O Lord. Stay with me as I continue to grow in your love and healing. Amen.

Listen! I am standing at the door, knocking; if you hear my voice and open the door, I will come in to you and eat with you, and you with me. *Revelation 3:20 NRSV*

I'm always a little bit curious when my doorbell rings or there's a knock at the door. Especially when I'm not expecting a visitor. I'm interested to see who is waiting on the other side. Perhaps it's an out-of-town friend stopping to say hello. Or maybe the delivery person has a package I need to sign for and accept.

Wouldn't it be great, if upon opening your door, there stood Jesus? What would you do? How would you react? After getting over the initial shock, hopefully you'd invite him inside. Would you busy yourself as Martha preparing a meal or sit quietly at his feet like Mary, drinking in his knowledge and love?

As believers, we have access to Jesus at any time. When you need a spirit of peace and calm in your life, invite him in. He will enter with a gentle smile and warm hug just for you.

Listen. Is someone knocking at your door?

Thank you, Lord, for being only "a knock away." Amen.

Consider what great things he has done for you.
1 Samuel 12:24b NRSV

When you look at a glass filled with water, what do you see? Is the glass half full or half empty? Your answer may reflect your outlook on life. Or are you detail oriented? Detail people, like myself, focus on the minute details instead of looking at the big picture.

Our human nature causes us to focus on the ugliness of life instead of the beauty. Yet we know in our hearts it should be the other way around.

Have you considered lately the blessings God has poured out for you? If not, take a few moments right now to reflect on the great things the Lord has done in your life. Then be sure to thank him.

Lord God, today I remember the good in my life. Help me continue to focus on the positives. Amen.

Serenity

Peace I leave with you; my peace I give to you. . . . Do not let your hearts be troubled, and do not let them be afraid.

John 14:27 NRSV

Several years ago a television commercial portrayed a harried woman trying to juggle life among her work, home and family. Her solution? You would find her soaking in a warm, soothing tub using the sponsor's bath product. Somehow the advertising executives wanted us to believe that the tub and its contents could whisk us away to another world.

Of course, taking time to relax in warm, whirling waters is helpful. Eating chocolate or shopping at the mall may temporarily soothe our troubles and fears. But are those good choices to help us cope in our fast-paced world?

What should our solution be to a hurried life? When we find ourselves rushing around, we need to remind ourselves to slow down, stop and think.

To find lasting satisfaction, seek out the wellspring of living water. Look to Jesus for his promise of peace in your life.

Continue to come into my life, Jesus. I humbly ask for your peace and grace. Amen.

As for me and my household, we will serve the Lord.
Joshua 24:15b NRSV

I wonder if Joshua knew how popular his words would become. Perhaps you've seen this scripture written on everything from paperweights to pictures. And if you were to visit my mother-in-law's home, you'd see Joshua 24:15 boldly inscribed on a large stone by her front door.

When Joshua spoke these words to the Israelites, he declared his loyalty and worship to the Lord. He reminded them of how the Lord had blessed their lives. Joshua asked them to make a choice. Which god will you choose to serve? The gods of your ancestors? Or the one, true God of Israel?

Our God—the same God of Joshua—gives us the free will to choose whom we will praise and worship.

Whom do you choose to serve this day? Remember the blessings the Lord has showered upon you.

Lord, I praise and thank you for your faithfulness. Amen.

If the offering is a sacrifice of well-being . . . you shall offer one without blemish before the Lord. *Leviticus 3:1 NRSV*

What does "well-being" mean to you? Do you think in terms of wellness—a popular word used today in fitness centers and the medical community? Does wellness encompass our physical, emotional and spiritual health?

To the Israelites the meaning was much different. The sacrifice of well-being was a way for them to give thanks and commune with God. It was also a peace offering to their Lord.

Today, we don't need to follow the Levitical rules of sacrificial grain or animals for the atonement of our sins. Jesus, who died for everyone, is our sacrificial lamb. By his death on the cross, we are a forgiven and redeemed people. Communion is possible at any time.

Yet, the Lord desires for us to give our hearts to him. When we approach him with our sacrificial hearts, he brings wholeness and peace.

Lord God, I desire nothing more than you. Daily I die to self and give my life to you. Amen.

A cheerful heart is a good medicine, but a downcast spirit dries up the bones. *Proverbs 17:22 NRSV*

Are there times when you find yourself more susceptible to illness? If you're around others who have the sniffles, are you likely to catch the same cold or flu?

We know the importance of eating properly and taking the right vitamins. Adequate rest and exercise also contribute to a healthy lifestyle. So, if we're doing all the right things, we should feel good about ourselves. Right? Well, maybe.

As the Holy Spirit fills you with peace, remember the importance of remaining optimistic. Focus on what is good in your life. Both your heart and outlook on life will benefit.

Put on a cheerful heart today. It will help you avoid those sniffles!

Jesus, continue to fill me with your cheerful spirit. Amen.

Serenity

O taste and see that the Lord is good; happy are those who take refuge in him. *Psalm 34:8 NRSV*

This verse from the Psalms was the theme for one of the first infertility conferences where I spoke. At the conference, I shared my story of loss, grief and healing. It was a special, grace-filled time in my life. Even in the midst of hurt and pain, those who attended the conference experienced a warm and loving weekend. Amidst their struggles was joy and serenity.

How has your "serenity gauge" been lately? Has life returned to some sort of normalcy? When we find our lives returning to a sense of order and daily routines, we often forget where our peace originated. In the busyness of our lives, we may unconsciously push aside the One who helped us through the valley.

Do you need a little refreshment in your life? Come to God's oasis. Taste and see his goodness and mercy. Let God's peace keep you steadfast in your daily walk with him.

Lord, since I've been better, I sometimes forget you. Forgive me and restore my dependence on you. Amen.

Let the little children come to me . . . for it is to such as these that the kingdom of heaven belongs. *Matthew 19:14 NRSV*

If you were to visit my church, you'd notice a plaque hanging on the wall as you walk into the nursery. It's not very large, and you need to get close to read the inscription. But it's a special plaque, especially to the parents who lovingly placed it there.

This plaque was given in memory of the parents' babies and children who had died. And what better words to use than Jesus' from Matthew 19. Our Jesus, who cares for everyone, promises to include our little children in his kingdom.

Does Jesus' promise bring you comfort? As he blessed and prayed for the little children in New Testament times, know that your little one receives the same blessing and care from him today.

Can you picture Jesus surrounded by little children and babies? What a marvelous sight!

Dear Jesus, I am at peace because I know my baby is with you. Amen.

Do you like honey? Don't eat too much of it, or it will make you sick! *Proverbs 25:16 TLB*

I love to eat. Especially anything that is "not healthy" for me. From sweets to crunchy, salty snacks and everything in between. And whenever I'm feeling stressed, there's nothing better than chocolate covered peanuts!

Okay, now that I've confessed my poor eating habits, how about you? Since your loss, how has your appetite fared? Are you eating properly? Perhaps you're eating in excess, like I tend to do when I'm stressed. Maybe you're not eating enough.

And what about exercise? Decide today to begin eating and exercising wisely. Ask a friend to help you. Or how about your spouse?

Remember, as you have come to wholeness, don't return to former unhealthy habits. Continue to take care of yourself: physically, emotionally and spiritually.

Lord God, you have created me in your image. Help me to be a good steward of my body. Amen.

So these stones shall be . . . a memorial forever.
Joshua 4:7b NRSV

Every parent in the support group had a unique story to tell about their loss. Some had experienced a stillbirth. Others had babies who had been sleeping, never to awake again. SIDS had snatched them away. Many had experienced the heartache of ectopic pregnancy or miscarriage.

Funerals and burials had been held for those babies who had lived longer in the womb or died after birth. Parents, especially moms, would share how they visited their sons' or daughters' gravesites. But for those parents who had experienced an early loss, there was no viable baby. No body to hold or bury. There was no closure, no resting place, no memorial to visit.

So the group of bereaved parents took action. With the generous donation from a monument company, a memorial marker was installed where moms and dads could come to remember their babies. It became a healing place where one could reflect and be restored.

If your baby died early in pregnancy, there are ways you can also honor his or her memory. You may choose to have a stone engraved and placed in your garden. Or select a living memorial--plant a tree or rose bush in memory of your baby. You may have other ideas as well.

Memorials of stone bring honor and respect for our babies whose lives have been taken too soon. What do these "stones" mean to you?

Father God, I long for a sacred place to remember my little one. Let it be a place that will bring honor to his memory. Amen.

For where two or three are gathered in my name, I am there among them. *Matthew 18:20 NRSV*

Caring for one another is more than just a suggestion for Christians. We're commanded to reach out to others with the love of Christ.

Have you had an opportunity to share God's love and care with someone who has also suffered a loss? Paul writes in Galatians we are to, "share each other's troubles and problems." *(6:2 TLB)*

Sometimes we might feel that if we're not helping the multitudes, our faith work is in vain. Yet, I'm glad Jesus spoke, "where two or more are gathered . . ." It reminds us that he is in our midst whether we minister to one person or to many.

Perhaps you're at the place where you can "step out" in faith and begin to help others. Have you been involved with a bereaved parent support group? If not, you may want to think about organizing a group at your church for those who have suffered the death of a child.

Are there other ways you can turn your grief experience into a growing experience for yourself and others?

Thank you, Father, for giving me the opportunity to reach out and help others who are hurting. Give me your wisdom to know what to do. Amen.

I will praise thee, for thou dost fill me with awe; wonderful thou art, and wonderful thy works. *Psalm 139:14 NEB*

It is good to be at the place of thankfulness and praise. When we can truly be thankful for the negatives in our lives, along with the positives, we know we have arrived.

Of course, there are times when we slip back into the old habits of feeling sorry for ourselves, complaining, not getting our own way. At these times, it is okay to acknowledge those emotions, work through them and place them again at the foot of the cross.

Delight in our awesome God, who brings you peace even during a storm. Take delight in him who has created the heavens and the earth. Give him thanks and praise today for your life!

I praise you, O God, for you are a God of goodness and mercy, who endures forever and forever. Amen.

For we cannot keep from speaking about what we have seen and heard. *Acts 4:20 NRSV*

Have you ever marveled at the resiliency and strength of someone who has endured difficult challenges in their life? Or overcome tremendous obstacles? There are times we look at others and wonder, "How did they survive?" Perhaps we believe we could never have gone through what they experienced.

What do you suppose your family and friends say about you? Do they see you as a survivor? After we pick up the pieces of our loss and grief, where do we stand? In the midst of the junk pile of bitterness and anger? Or in green pastures of peace?

It may all have to do with how we portray ourselves and communicate with those around us. While we can't testify to the sights and sounds Peter and John experienced with Jesus, we can share how Jesus has helped us through our grief.

When we emerge from hopelessness into wholeness again, we cannot help but speak about what we have seen and heard. By sharing our transformation story, we give God the glory.

Make it a point to tell others the wonderful things the Lord has done for you. Let them know you are a survivor.

How majestic is your name, O Lord! Open my mouth so I may speak of your healing power and love in my life. Amen.

He comforts us in all our troubles, so that we in turn may be able to comfort others in any trouble of theirs and to share with them the consolation we ourselves receive from God.

2 Corinthians 1:4 NEB

I love the imagery of God as a comforter. Can't you just feel yourself wrapped in his loving arms like a warm, soft, cuddly blanket? Being comforted is a gift from heaven. It's the hand and heart of God working through his people.

People who comfort are so very important to us. How I wish there would have been a comforter in my life after my first pregnancy loss.

Since your baby died, has there been someone special who has comforted you? If so, thank God for that person now. Better yet, write a note expressing your thankfulness. Let that person know how you appreciate being helped through your sorrow.

As we receive gifts of care and consolation, we shouldn't keep them to ourselves. There *will* come a time when others will look to you for the same understanding you received from your special comforter.

At that time, you will understand how your loss can be transformed from despair to hope. *From sorrow to serenity.*

Thank you, Lord, for your compassion and care. Help me to know who I can reach out to with your love and comfort. Amen.

And the peace of God, which surpasses all understanding, will guard your hearts and your minds in Christ Jesus.

Philippians 4:7 NRSV

Somewhere along the journey of our grief we realize we have changed. We cannot experience death and expect any less. Like the butterfly emerging from its chrysalis, we, too, are a transformed people. Yet, has our transformation been for the better or worse?

As redeemed and forgiven children of God, we are given the right to choose. When tragedy strikes, we can choose to become bitter or better. My choice has been to become better. At the time of my mourning, I would not have thought it possible to be thankful to God for placing me in the midst of seven years of repeated pregnancy loss. But in those seven years, I was also given hope. The hope of God's peace. Even though I didn't understand from an earthly perspective why bad things were happening, God's comfort encompassed me.

Dear sisters and brothers in Christ, continue to choose the path marked love and grace, no matter what your future brings. Embrace the peace of God in your lives forever . . .

Heavenly Father, thank you for guiding me through my loss and pain and into a new life of peace. I will continue to walk with you, wherever you lead. Amen.

Special Days

This is the day
that the Lord has made;
let us rejoice and
be glad in it.

Psalm 118:24 NRSV

New Year's Day

You crown the year with your bounty.

Psalm 65:11a NRSV

Happy New Year!

Perhaps it's not so happy for you as another year begins. You may be thinking, "What do I have to look forward to?" or "Happy? What's there to be happy about? My baby just died."

If it has been some time since your loss, you may well be on the road to healing. If your loss has been more recent, however, you may still find yourself struggling to climb out of the muck and mire of grief.

And with the new year, comes those wonderful New Year's resolutions. If you were to make a resolution, what would it be? The "eat healthier, exercise more" resolution many of us make only to break a few weeks later?

What would deepen your spiritual life and bring you closer to God? Devoting more time to read scripture and spending more time in prayer may be two ways. Perhaps reaching out to others who are suffering or trying to be more positive are others.

There are many ways each of us can respond to God in this new year. Today, ask the Lord what you can do for him. Then wait to see how he showers his abundant love upon you.

Lord God, you create each day as a new day. As a new year begins, help me focus on the goodness and mercy you have for me and in my life. Amen.

Easter
The Death and Resurrection of Jesus

See, I am making all things new.

Revelation 21:5a NRSV

Christ is risen! He is risen indeed!

Throughout the Easter season, the above greeting and response is enthusiastically spoken at my church. After spending forty days observing Lent and reflecting on our spiritual lives, we joyfully celebrate. Like the sun emerging from behind ominous clouds, the children of God spring forth from darkness into the light.

As we celebrate Easter today, are you surrounded by clouds of darkness? Do you wonder if and when you will ever escape from your sadness and enter into the light again?

Others before us have wondered as well. Two thousand years ago on that first Easter, Jesus' disciples questioned. Amidst grief, their savior and friend was dead. Could they really believe in a resurrection?

And what do you—one who has struggled through the grief of losing your baby—believe? Can you continue to believe in a loving Father who promises never to leave his children?

No matter where you are on your grief journey, keep faith in your Heavenly Father's promise of the resurrection of his son, Jesus. Take heart knowing that your little one is safe in the arms of Jesus.

Father God, I give you all praise and honor and glory for the gift of your resurrected son, Jesus the Christ. Alleluia! Amen.

He will gather the lambs in his arms.

Isaiah 40:11b NRSV

Do I have to get out of bed today, Lord? Will you forgive me if I don't attend church? I'm not sure I can bear the thought of all those moms and babies being honored during the worship service this morning.

Yes, the celebration of Mother's Day may bring forth many different emotions you hadn't expected. Anticipation of flowers, cards, slobbery kisses and chubby arms hugging your neck are denied. Thinking of "what should have been" may bring tears, sadness and anger. Even if you have other children at home, you still may feel sadness that part of your family is missing.

Please remember that even though your baby isn't physically with you, you are still a mom. You have been given a precious gift to cherish forever.

As you give thanks for your mother, thank the Lord for giving you the gift of your baby—no matter how long he or she lived. Mom, *you* are special to him, and you are special to your little one.

Mother me today, Lord. Gather me in your tender, loving arms and gently rock me. Amen.

Father's Day

O Lord, all my longing is known to you; my sighing is not hidden from you. *Psalm 38:9 NRSV*

Is today a day you have been longing for or dreading? Perhaps you weren't sure whether to anticipate or dismiss this day that honors fathers. Would it be easier to focus your attention on your father instead of remembering that you are a childless father? Then you won't have to deal with your own loss.

Today you may think about all the opportunities you might have shared with your son or daughter as they grew. Vivid scenes may appear in your mind. Can you see yourself playing catch or helping him ride his bike without training wheels or building her first doll house?

Many husbands need to recognize the loss of their baby. Yet sometimes they deny their grief by shifting their focus to support their wives. Too often, men push their hurt and pain aside to "be strong" for their spouse. While this is admirable, it is also unhealthy. Fathers need to acknowledge their pain and not deprive themselves of ways in which to heal their sorrow.

So today make a point to acknowledge your feelings of loss. Ask yourself if you can share your thoughts with your spouse. Or write a letter or poem about your baby. Expressing and releasing your thoughts through the written word can restore an empty heart.

On this Father's Day, know that your Father in heaven is with you. He understands your loss, your longings and your sighs. Let him care for you today. Feel his comfort, peace and healing wash over you.

There is nothing I can keep from you, Lord. Help me understand and accept the loss of my baby. Amen.

Rejoice always, pray without ceasing, give thanks in all circumstances; for this is the will of God in Christ Jesus for you.
1 Thessalonians 5:16-18 NRSV

It has been too easy to focus on what I do not have rather than what I am blessed with. And it has taken a long time to turn the "thanklessness" into "thankfulness." I never thought I would be thankful for six pregnancies that never made it to term.

But God, through his Holy Spirit, works in mysterious ways. And God's Spirit has been prodding, coaxing me in a silent, yet remarkable fashion.

I am truly thankful for those little babes. Only they know how their short lives have affected, changed me forever. They have made me grow in ways I could not have begun to imagine just a few years ago. Because of their deaths, opportunities to share and minister to other bereaved parents have opened up. New friendships have come into my life—soul sisters and brothers who share the pain and recovery of our unfair losses.

I miss them. Bittersweet thoughts come to mind when I think what it could have been like had my babies lived. My focus now tries to be not on what I am missing but on the joyous reunion I will have with them one day.

For that I am thankful.

Father, I admit there are many times I am not thankful. I honestly thank you for the trials and the blessings. Thank you for my family. Amen.

Christmas Day

Today in the city of David a deliverer has been born to you—the Messiah, the Lord. *Luke 2:11 NEB*

The Christmas holiday season can be an extremely painful time for bereaved parents. It is a holiday where children seem to be the center of attention. And some decisions that have been easy for you to make in the past become more difficult.

For instance, how should we sign our Christmas cards? If we don't include our baby as a part of our family, it will seem like she never existed. What about baby's stocking, lovingly made, ready to hang? Or the "Baby's First Christmas" ornament for the tree? Do we have to gather together with the entire family? Know that there are no right or wrong answers. Decide what feels right and comfortable for you.

Yet we know Christmas is also the time to focus on the birth of another baby. Over the years, I've encountered bereaved parents who couldn't joyfully celebrate the birth of God's son when their baby had died. Christmas to them was a cruel reminder of what they physically didn't have.

How about you? If this is the first Christmas since your baby died, it will no doubt be difficult. Sometimes anticipation is worse than what may happen on Christmas day. So plan something special for you and your spouse. Attend worship services at a different church. Or read *The Christmas Miracle of Jonathan Toomey* by Susan Wojciechoswski, while you snuggle together sipping hot cider. Whatever your plans for this holy day, be gentle with yourselves.

Jesus, as I celebrate your birth, a part of my family is missing. Fill the void in my life with your spirit of peace, joy and love. Amen.

The memory of the righteous is a blessing.

Proverbs 10:7a NRSV

Is it difficult to believe a year has passed since your little one died? Our days, weeks and months meld together when we journey through the darkness of grief.

One year ago you were dealt with an unspeakable death. Did you believe you could survive the pain and anguish? As a survivor, realize the important milestone you have reached along the path of life.

Proverbs reminds us that our babies, whether born or unborn when they died, are counted among the blessed righteous in the sight of God. We need to remember them as the blessings they are and will continue to be in our lives.

Do you have special plans today to commemorate your baby? You might consider taking the day off from work to spend with your spouse or giving a gift to a children's ministry in your baby's name. Don't be afraid to let family and friends know what would be of help to you. Choose what feels right for you and will bring honor to your baby and glory and praise to God.

As you celebrate a different kind of anniversary today, remember the essence of life your baby gave to you. Recall how your little one has changed your life—how God continues to mold you as you come out of the darkness and into his glorious light.

Heavenly Father, I will never forget my baby. As I remember my little one today, fill me with your peace and continue to keep my baby in your care. Amen.

Resource Centers

Stepping Stones
901 Eastern Avenue NE
P. O. Box 294
Grand Rapids, MI 49501-0294
(616) 224-7488 or (616) 224-7529
www.bethany.org/stepping/ e-mail: step@bethany.org

Offering Christian hope, encouragement and support for those experiencing infertility and pregnancy and infant loss.

Pregnancy and Infant Loss Center
1421 E. Wayzata Blvd., #30
Wayzata, MN 55391-1939
(612) 473-9372

Providing support, resources and education on miscarriage, stillbirth and infant death.

National SHARE Office
St. Joseph Health Center
300 First Capitol Drive
St. Charles, MO 63301-2893
(314) 947-6164 or 1-800-821-6819
www.nationalShareOffice.com
e-mail: SHARE@NationalSHAREOffice.com

To touch those who are touched by the tragic death of a baby through miscarriage, stillbirth or newborn death.

Perinatal Loss
2116 NE 18th Avenue
Portland, OR 97212
(503) 284-7426
www.teleport.com/~grieving/index.htm
e-mail: grieving@teleport.com

Offering bereavement resources for perinatal loss.

RESOLVE
1310 Broadway
Somerville, MA 02144
(617) 623-0744 — National Help Line
www.resolve.org

Assisting people in resolving their infertility by providing information, support and advocacy.

American SIDS Institute
6065 Roswell Road, Suite 876
Atlanta, GA 30328
(404) 843-1030
www.sids.org
e-mail: prevent@sids.org

Dedicated to the prevention of SIDS and the promotion of infant health through research, clinical services, family support and professional and community education.

SIDS Alliance
1314 Bedford Avenue, Suite 210
Baltimore, MD 21208
1-800-221-SIDS (Information & Referral Hotline)
www.sidsalliance.org
e-mail: sidshq@charm.net

Dedicated to the support of SIDS families, education and research.

The Compassionate Friends
P. O. Box 3696
Oak Brook, IL 60522-3696
(630) 990-0010
www.compassionatefriends.org
e-mail: TCF_National@prodigy.com

Offering friendship and understanding to families who are grieving the death of a child of any age from any cause.

About the Author

Susan Fletcher writes and speaks from her experience of infertility, repeated pregnancy loss, adoption and family life. She has also written extensively for both the children's and adult devotional markets. She resides in Cedar Rapids, Iowa, with her husband and two sons. *From Sorrow to Serenity* is her first book.

To order additional copies of *From Sorrow to Serenity* please send check or money order for $8.95 plus $2.00 for shipping and handling, for a total of $10.95 per book. Iowa residents please add 5% sales tax.

Please make checks payable to: Susan Fletcher

Send to: Susan Fletcher
513 Knollwood Drive SE
Cedar Rapids, IA 52403

To schedule the author for speaking engagements, please write to: 513 Knollwood Drive SE
Cedar Rapids, IA 52403